Song of Songs

An Alternative View

I0162829

By Sylvia Penny

ISBN: 978-1-78364-537-4

www.obt.org.uk

Unless indicated otherwise Scripture quotations are taken from the Holy Bible, New International Version Anglicised Copyright © 1979, 1984, 2011 Biblica. Used by permission of Hodder & Stoughton Ltd, an Hachette UK company. All rights reserved. 'NIV' is a registered trademark of Biblica UK trademark number 1448790.

****

THE OPEN BIBLE TRUST
Fordland Mount, Upper Basildon,
Reading, RG8 8LU, UK

Song of Songs

An Alternative View

Contents

Page

Section One

An alternative view of The Song of Songs

An alternative view of The Song of Songs

Much has been written about the Song of Songs over the centuries. Theories abound as to its true meaning. These include:

1. It is a collection of love poems, and should be understood literally.

2. It is a drama with three main characters, Solomon, the maiden and her rustic lover, and various other lesser characters.

3. For the Jews in the past it has been taken as an allegory describing God's dealings with His people Israel.

4. For Christians today, it has been understood as the Lord's love for His Church.

This simply illustrates how difficult it is, first to understand this book, and second to understand why it is included in the Canon of Scripture. On this second point the *New Bible Commentary Revised (page 579)* states "the fact that it probably owes its existence in the Canon to an allegorical interpretation is still no basis for the acceptance of such an interpretation". I would agree. *Peake's Commentary* states that "there is nothing in the poems which suggests that they are allegories".

I do not intend to go into these various scenarios, as this has already been done very well by Brian Sherring in his booklet "The Greatest Love Song", followed by a verse by verse commentary on the entire book. However, what I would like to do here is to put forward an alternative view on how to understand this short book. As stated above, I agree that it should be understood literally, and not allegorically, and that it should be allowed to take its natural interpretation. It presents itself as a series of beautifully expressed love poems (or songs), and I believe these should be taken at face value. However, if we do that, then the question as to why God wished this to be included in Scripture is a valid one.

Many follow variations of the second theory stated above. It is a story, or a drama, told in poetic form, of a man and a woman deeply in love, in a monogamous relationship, possibly betrothed to each other, waiting for their wedding day. However, there are a number of details within the Song that sit uneasily with this interpretation, and which, in my view, do not quite "fit". Imaginative explanations have often been used in order to support this scenario, or variations on it.

I have therefore tried to come up with a scenario which answers as many of the difficulties (as I see them) as possible. One person's introduction to the Song states that each person should approach this book and study it for themselves, as it is impossible to be definitive about its precise meaning in many places. There is room for differences of opinion on who is speaking, how many characters there are, whether or not Solomon himself features, and what is meant by certain words and phrases. What follows, therefore, is simply my view of a possible structure for the Song. It takes into account what many others have said, and finds a way of looking at it which seeks to explain some of the problems that otherwise arise.

One of the keys to understanding this book is the fact that it is poetry, that there are repetitions and refrains throughout, and that these should be harmonised if we are to understand what is being said. If it is accepted to be a series of poems, even if they are separately identifiable, it has been pointed out they also form a cohesive whole as a book. Even if they were not all written by the same person, it is most likely that they were collated skilfully by one person, and specifically arranged in order to produce a final overall composition. And we should not overlook the fact that all of Scripture is written under the inspiration of the Holy Spirit, and as such must have been included in the Canon in the way it has been for a very good reason.

In my view, the Song can be looked at as describing the relationships between four different, individual women with four different men - one with a king, one with Solomon, one with an unfaithful lover, and one with a faithful lover. These are set out below:

The Women	The Men
1. Concubine	1. King
2. Suntanned girl; the Shulammite	2. Unfaithful lover
3. Royal bride; a virgin	3. Solomon
4. Girl in a house; "prince's daughter", chaste lover	4. Faithful lover

These are compared and contrasted with one another throughout the Song. Each couple appears in two or more sections of the book, and I have listed the verses that refer to each couple below. When the book is read in this way, the repetitions and descriptions for each couple become apparent, and are consistent one with another. We also have an explanation for the refrain, recorded three times in this book, "do not arouse or awaken love until it so desires." (2:7; 3:5; 8:4). If the entire book were about one perfect, monogamous couple, then it seems strange this refrain is emphasised and repeated. Rather, it warns and adjures the "daughters of Jerusalem" *not* to arouse or awaken love (i.e. "excite the passions" – see *Companion Bible*) – not exactly what one would expect from a happily betrothed woman awaiting her wedding day! Instead, this is more fitting for a girl who has been left by her lover, who has gone off to pastures new. There are a number of such *seeming* inconsistencies in this book that need to be explained in some way, but if there are four couples, not one, these problems disappear.

Why would four couples be included by the author? There are parallels and contrasts between each two pairs of couples. First, the king has many concubines, just as the unfaithful lover has many women. Second, Solomon has only one royal bride (only in this poem, not in reality) just as the faithful lover has eyes for only one girl, and he refers to her as a "prince's daughter". The two pairs of couples are therefore both balanced and contrasted in the Song. The purity of the faithful lovers' relationship shines out against the others, as do the beautiful poems that describe their love and longing for each other.

Why is this book included in Scripture? Various commentators have pointed out that it is unique in Scripture as it is the only book that deals solely with the love between men and women, and this it does beautifully. The *New Bible Commentary Revised* says "it is a song of great beauty and power with delicately chosen imagery from field and garden, animal life and plant life." However, it is not only an incomparable piece of literature on human love, it also serves as a warning to women not to "arouse love before it so desires". Women will be hurt and disillusioned by men if they arouse expectations in them and consummate their love early in their relationship (2:3-4). Some men, who act like the kings in the OT with their harems (1:2; 1:4), will go from woman to woman (3:1; 5:8; 6:1; 6:2), leaving the women to regret encouraging such a relationship (2:7; 3:5; 8:4), which to the man may be based mainly on physical attraction. On the other hand, women will be esteemed and respected by men, if they remain chaste before their wedding day, like the royal bride with King Solomon. The physical attraction is still very much there, but is consummated at the right time, on the wedding night (see 4:16; 5:1; 8:12). Physical attraction between men and women is not wrong, but the Song of Songs in the Bible warns that the consummation of this should be unique between one man and one woman, reserved for one monogamous relationship of mutual love and trust. In this context, physical love between a man and a woman is seen to be a beautiful thing, designed by God and resulting in a totally unique relationship, different from all others, throughout the couple's life. The couple become, and remain, truly "one" in the eyes of God (Genesis 2:24; Matthew 19:5). The Song of Songs is not only relevant to the age in which it was written, but, as human nature does not change over the centuries, I believe it is just as relevant today.

Suggested Structure of the Song of Songs

Each of the four couples' poems can be read in the order given below, which will then give the reader an idea of how the same phrases and themes are repeated for each of these couples. This is particularly so for the Shulammite, and for the "girl in a house". The concubine and the royal bride can also be compared and contrasted easily, as there are only two sections for each of these two couples.

In section 3 of this booklet I have set out in detail the *reasons* for allocating to each couple the particular verses selected below.

However, for now they have simply been stated without any supporting explanations. This is in order to give a clear overview of the entire Song to start with, before dealing with the detailed analysis showing how I arrived at the divisions suggested.

(1) **Concubine and king** - 1:1-4; 1:9-15

> The concubine understands her position. She knows she is one of many, and this was simply accepted as part of royal society in the culture of that time. It is neither condemned nor condoned in the Song. It is included as a parallel and a contrast to the Shulammite. The similarity is that she loves the king, and he enjoys her beauty. The contrast is that she *knows* she is not the only one and had no expectations of being so. Also, she had no choice in her position, so she just had to make the best of it.

(2) **Shulammite and her unfaithful lover** – 1:5-8; 1:16-2:7; 3:1-5;5:2-6:2; 6:11-13; 8:1-4; 8:5b

> The Shulammite's love for her lover seems to be one sided. She is faint with love for him, whereas although he is interested in her in the beginning, he loses interest after their love is consummated (2:4). As a result, she warns the daughters of Jerusalem three times not to arouse or awaken physical love in a man until the right time. Unlike the concubine, she has chosen to be with her lover, but when he chooses to leave her, she regrets giving him her love so soon. Unlike the "girl in a house" she is not a "wall" – i.e. chaste, but a "door" – i.e. of easy virtue. She would have done better had she remained "enclosed". She gave away "her vineyard" at the wrong time, and far too soon, unlike the chaste "girl in a house" who waits for her wedding day.

Her story stands as a valuable lesson for all women, whenever and wherever they have lived, on how to avoid hurt and heartache.

(3) **Royal bride and Solomon** – 3:6-11; 4:8-5:1

The royal bride contrasts with the concubine. In the poem she is depicted as special to him, and *not* just one among many. The royal couple are happy enough with each other when they meet. She steals his heart with one glance of her eyes (4:9), and she is happy to accept his words of praise and his overtures to her (4:16). However, there are no long and loving poems expressing their deeply held feelings and longings, as there are between the "girl in a house" and her faithful lover. There is no physical relationship until they are married, and in the royal culture of that time their betrothal and marriage is carried out properly and in accordance with the customs of that time.

(4) **Girl in a house and her faithful lover** – 2:8-17; 4:1-7; 6:3-10; 7:1-13; 8:5a; 8:6-14

The "girl in a house" and her faithful lover stand for God's ideal for men and women. They have a mutual love and respect for one another, they conduct themselves appropriately, they express their deepest feelings for one another, but they wait until their wedding day before they express their love in a physical way. The similarity between this couple and the royal couple's relationships is that they are conducted correctly and in accordance with God's moral law. The contrast between the two couples is the way in which their love is expressed. This faithful couple have got to know each other and fallen in love. It is not a relationship that has been arranged for political or other reasons. The level of spontaneous, joyful and romantic love expressed between these two, as a result, is so much greater. The description of love given in 8:6-7 is superlative, where the "girl in a house" says that love is as strong as death, it burns like a blazing fire, it is like a mighty flame that many waters cannot quench, and that rivers cannot wash it away. Theirs is an emotional and all-encompassing love that dwarfs all others, and sweeps them both away!

By weaving these poems together in the way they have been, the comparisons and contrasts are carefully and tastefully expressed. They give the overall message that God wants the physical union between man and woman to be reserved for a life-long monogamous relationship, and that nothing else can compare with this. This leads to complete satisfaction and contentment, and a deep and lasting love, rather than broken relationships, hurt feelings, and heartache.

Section Two

A consideration of the "shepherd hypothesis" in The Song of Songs

A consideration of the "shepherd hypothesis" in The Song of Songs

Having set out my alternative view to understanding the Song of Songs in section one, here in section two I have set out a brief summary of one popular understanding of the Song, the "shepherd hypothesis". I then set out the reasons I find it difficult to accept this view and go on to explain how my alternative view takes into account some of these problems and difficulties.

Briefly, the "shepherd hypothesis" puts forward the view that there are two main lovers in the Song, a shepherd and a Shulammite girl, between whom there is a genuine and pure love. Solomon however captures the Shulammite girl for his harem and attempts to win her affection, but he is unsuccessful.

Peake's Commentary states that "this explanation requires much ingenuity in assigning the poems to the characters" and I would have to agree with this. There seems to be a number of problems with this scenario.

1. The first problem is that it casts Solomon in a bad light. He steps in between two devoted lovers and attempts to destroy their relationship by winning her affection for himself instead. Not only this, he is then ultimately unsuccessful. On both counts this seems unlikely to me. Although some

dispute that Solomon was the author, it is generally thought that if he was not, then it was attributed to him by another person who collated the entire Song and dedicated it to him at a later date. Whichever view we accept, however, it seems unlikely that Solomon would cast himself in such a bad light, but it also seems unlikely someone else would do so. People sometimes ascribed their own work to famous figures in the past in order to gain credence for their own writings. If that is the case, they are highly unlikely to denigrate that person in the eyes of others.

This understanding of the Song is, however, thought to be more likely than the view that Solomon was writing about a devoted relationship between *himself* and the Shulammite, because he could hardly be considered a good example of true, loyal, and exclusive love in the light of his 700 wives and 300 concubines (1 Kings 11:1-3), and this I would have to agree with. However, on reading the Song through in a number of different translations, the "shepherd hypothesis" raises too many questions for me to accept that this is in fact what the book is about.

2. If only *one* lover features in the Song, then this "shepherd lover" is also referred to as a "king" in chapter one (1:4; 1:12). If there is only one girl in the Song, then she is variously described as looking after her family's vineyards (1:6), possessing expensive gold and silver jewellery (1:10), being a bride from Lebanon (4:8), and a Shulammite (6:13). It seems unlikely that a country girl would be rich enough to own expensive jewellery, and it also seems unlikely that she was both Lebanese and a Shulammite. So, in order to explain these anomalies, it is usually stated that

these are poetic ways of describing how they saw each other.

3. Physical love is expressed from the outset (1:2, 4, 13, 16). Consummation of love is alluded to shortly after (2:3-7). Yet 4:12 implies the girl is still a virgin, and only *afterwards* is their love consummated (4:16-5:1). Again, in the last chapter, the girl is described as chaste (8:10, 12). Flashbacks and/or looking forward to the future are often invoked in order to explain these passages. Alternatively, it is denied that this is what these verses refer to, and they are instead given an alternative, sanitised meaning, despite many such commentaries also admitting that this book contains "apparent eroticism" (e.g. *New Bible Commentary Revised*).

However, if we take the view, as I have suggested in section one, that there are four pairs of lovers, then all such explanations are unnecessary. There are no problems with Solomon being cast in a bad light, as in my alternative scenario he is not. There are no problems with the "shepherd lover" being described as "a king" in chapter one, nor the rustic maiden possessing jewellery she could never have afforded, when we see that these passages are describing different lovers and different girls. There are also no problems with the lovers' consummation described early in the book, only to find them awaiting this on their wedding day later on. It all falls into place if we see these are in fact *different* couples.

Section Three

Reasons to believe that four couples are spoken of in The Song of Songs

Reasons to believe that four couples are spoken of in The Song of Songs

As mentioned in section one, the detailed analysis of the Song below is simply my view of a *possible* structure for the Song. But it also takes into account what a variety of commentators have said, and finds a way of looking at it which seeks to answer some of the problems that otherwise arise.

As in section one, I have separated the book under four headings, one for each of the couples. Under these headings I have again given the details of the verses which relate to each couple. However, this time, instead of simply *stating* this is the case, I have given the *reasons* for selecting the verses given for each couple and how I arrived at this structure for the book. I have not given a verse by verse commentary, as much of the longer sections of poetry can be understood by using the structure suggested below.

Before we look at the details, one question that may reasonably be asked is why the writer, or editor, did not set this book out as four separate continuous accounts to make for easy reading and instruction, rather than weaving them together as they have been. The answer to this rests upon the fact that the Song is considered by a number of commentators to comprise a number of poems, some of whom consider there to be as many as nineteen poems. This is stated in *Peake's Commentary*:

If we accept unity of authorship, it is reasonable to expect some progression of thought, although in the view of many the book consists of a collection of unconnected love poems. It is possible, however, to trace a movement of thought from courtship to marriage in the mind of the poet. ... We cannot always be confident where the individual poems begin and end, and therefore of the number of poems contained in the book. It will appear that we have distinguished some nineteen poems, but some of the divisions are perhaps arbitrary.

Here it is admitted that it is notoriously difficult to tell where one piece of writing ends, and another begins. Some even believe there is no consistent train of thought at all. However, I agree with *Peake's Commentary* in that I do see a movement of thought throughout, *not* an unconnected collection of poems.

Peake's Commentary also states:

(The Song) is a series of poems celebrating the love of a man and a woman. We may find in these poems a progression leading to love's consummation in marriage, and the depth and intensity of love itself is acknowledged. We shall not look for any particular man and woman whose love is being described. Rather we shall hear the words of a great poet who has chosen this medium for presenting the simplicity and the greatness, the gentleness and strength of love. The scenes he describes did not necessarily exist as he speaks of them; neither did the people he referred to have objective reality.

Although I agree with the generality of what is said, I see four couples rather than just one couple. Also, *Peake's Commentary* considers that the progression seen in the Song relates to the subject of *love itself*. However, I see comparisons and contrasts being made between four couples in order to show the best, and the worst, of human love within the relationships of these four very different couples.

So, we return to the question, if there are four couples, why did the author not set these poems out as four separate continuous accounts to make for easy reading and instruction? Part of my answer is that, if it is talking of just one couple, we might well ask the same question! Why did the author not make it clearer of whom he was speaking and why does it appear to be a series of unconnected thoughts (in some people's view). Also, *if* it is just one couple, how do we explain the anomalies that arise as a result (see section 2)? There are difficulties whichever way we look at it.

Also, we have to accept that this is a book of poetry, and as such, there are repetitions and refrains throughout that we should try to harmonise as much as possible if we are to understand the message. And we should not overlook the fact that all of Scripture is written under the inspiration of the Holy Spirit, and as such this must have been included in the Canon, and written in the way it has been, for a very good reason.

Lastly, if we compare the Song with the other writings attributed to King Solomon, (i.e. Proverbs and Ecclesiastes), we will find it is similarly difficult to follow the themes and trains of thought throughout these other two books. They also appear to be disjointed and difficult to understand in places. To our modern western minds, the wisdom and sayings in both of these books could have been collected together in a way that would make them more accessible and comprehensible to us today. However, the fact that they are not should not deter us from studying them and trying to understand and accept them as they are. The same is true of the Song.

In order to understand what is said it may be helpful to have a modern translation of the Song of Songs open while reading through this. The summaries of the verses given below are based on the NIV.

Detailed comments on the four couples in the Song of Songs

(1) The concubine and the king

1:1-4   The Song starts with her wanting the "kisses of his mouth"; she is one among many maidens; she goes to the king's chambers; the harem delight in the king; he is like a modern celebrity, and the concubine is not surprised the harem adore him.

The Song begins with a concubine, and a rich and powerful king. Some commentaries agree that the maidens are part of a royal harem, and that here they express their love for the king together with the concubine who is speaking in this section. This avoids re-interpreting the king as a "shepherd lover" and the girl as a virgin awaiting her wedding day, and trying to explain what it means by the king taking her into his inner chambers. The verses can simply be taken at face value. It is then a *different* girl who speaks, in verses 5-8, a suntanned girl who is lovely, and who is referred to as the Shulammite later in the Song.

The Song then returns to the concubine and the king:

1:9-15	The king speaks to the concubine and likens her to a mare among stallions; he praises the way she looks, and says he will make her more jewellery of gold and silver; the concubine describes the king reclining on his couch and she praises his charms; he tells her how beautiful she is.

These two sections contain two of the only three verses in the Song that refer to "the king". The third one comes in 7:5 where it forms a part of a standard bridal song. (In chapter 3, King Solomon is named specifically, but in these other three verses it just refers to "the king".) These verses describe the physical love between him and the concubine. The king has taken the concubine into his chambers, and reclines on his couch with her in attendance. Although this is translated "table" in the NIV, other translations have "couch" as the word "indicates some sort of semi-circular divan; probably a reclining seat", according to the *New Bible Commentary*.

To be part of a harem was to be part of an accepted and normal way of life in a royal court and there was no shame in it. The fact that she finds him attractive and he is pleased with her appearance is made clear by their words to each other. Therefore, the scene is set for the entire book from the very first sentence. "Let him kiss me with the kisses of his mouth" is how it starts, and this should not be forgotten when trying to understand what is being said throughout the rest of the book. Their physical love was acceptable within the royal courts at that time. Even King David, Solomon's father, possessed a harem and he was never condemned for this by the Lord. However, although it was accepted, it was not the Lord's ideal for men and women. As we read further in the Song of Songs, the contrast with the other three couples becomes clear.

(2) The Shulammite and her unfaithful lover

I refer to this girl as the "Shulammite" for ease of reference but, in fact, she is called by this name in just one verse, later in the Song (6:13).

1:5-8   She describes herself as suntanned yet lovely; she works in the vineyards; she does not know where her lover goes at midday, whereas his friends do, and they tell her where to find him.

In verse 5, the scene and mood change totally. Gone are the kisses, the fragrance of the king's perfume, the king's chamber, and the other maidens. Instead, this girl addresses "the daughters of Jerusalem" and also talks about her mother and brothers. She describes herself as darkened by the sun, but lovely even so! She works in the vineyards, but she does not know where her lover is. She has to ask his friends where to find him, and go in search of him. In other words, this girl pursues her lover, not the other way round. Therefore, from the outset this does not sound like a long-standing or a secure relationship, otherwise she would know where her lover was to be found, and surely if he was keen on her, *he* would be looking for *her*.

Verse 7 implies that she does *not* wear a veil. It is suggested by many commentaries that the reason she is described as "dark" is for this very reason. Without a veil, she has been darkened by the sun. Yet we see later, in 4:1 & 3 and 6:7 that the girl in *these* verses *does* wear a veil. Therefore, I believe, these later verses are instead referring to a *different* girl – a veiled girl who is the "faithful girl in a house". The veil helps to give an indication of her propriety in contrast to the Shulammite.

So, in these first few verses which introduce the Shulammite to us, we learn she does not care to veil herself. Maybe this is due to pride in her own appearance (v5 – "I am dark but lovely"). She is the only girl who refers to her *own* looks in the Song. This is the first hint we have of her lack of propriety, and also a touch of vanity. She protests that people stare at her, and yet on the other hand she protests at wearing a veil! Later, in 6:13, we also see that others ask her to come back, *four times*, so they can "gaze at her". Is she dressed in a certain way that provokes this response? We are also told that her "mother's sons", i.e. her brothers, were angry with her, but no reason is given. The reader is left to fill in the missing pieces.

We also find, as we go through the sections that refer to the Shulammite and her unfaithful lover, that it is only in these passages that "the daughters of Jerusalem" are addressed (see 1:5; 2:7; 3:5; 5:8; 5:16; 8:4). The repetition of this phrase helps to confirm that the girl being referred to in these sections of the Song is indeed the Shulammite. There is a consistency throughout in the way she refers to her friends and neighbours around her.

1:16-2:7   The girl and her lover are out in the woods together; her lover is like an apple tree and his fruit is sweet to her taste; the consummation of their love; her warning to the daughters of Jerusalem.

Although verse 16 mirrors verse 15, I believe a new section starts at verse 16 because the "verdant bed" would seem to describe a leafy or grassy woodland glade where this couple are lying, rather than a reclining couch in a bedroom chamber. The Shulammite girl almost repeats what the king says to the concubine in verse 15, so there is a stark contrast between the two relationships. The *king* praises the concubine's beauty in verse 15, whereas it is the *Shulammite* who praises how handsome and charming her lover is in verse 16. The *New Bible Commentary* maintains that here the girl is *thinking* of her "shepherd lover" in verse 16 while she is, in fact, with the king in his chamber (verse 15). It therefore recognises the complete change in tone and setting here and tries to explain this by suggesting these are her *thoughts*. It seems more likely that this is, in fact, a different girl, with a different lover.

The only praise this unfaithful lover gives the Shulammite is in 2:2, where she is "a lily among thorns" – which is not very flattering to the other maidens, as they are obviously the "thorns" in his opinion! Neither is he particularly extravagant in his praise of her.

Verses 3-6 are a tasteful expression of the consummation of their love out in the woods. Again the *New Bible Commentary* comments that the "banquet hall" could simply be "a house of love". This is followed by the final verse of the section where the girl adjures the "daughters of Jerusalem not to arouse or awaken love until it so desires". As already mentioned, this is stated three times in the Song. This helps in determining which parts of the Song relate to the Shulammite, as each time this phrase occurs, it is at the *end* of a section about her (unrequited) love. She warns other women in general not to do what she has done. She has been too free and easy with her love, only to be left by her unfaithful lover. This is in contrast to the concubine who is safe and secure in her situation – where even though it was obviously not God's ideal, neither was it condemned in their society.

Most commentaries see a clear break between verse 7 and verse 8. In fact, after each of the three times where the girl warns the daughters of Jerusalem, there is a clear break, and the following verse starts a new subject. Each time this happens, I believe a different couple starts the next section with a separate poem (i.e. 2:8; 3:6; 8:5).

3:1-5   The Shulammite has a dream: her lover has gone; she finds him and takes him to her mother's house; she warns the daughters of Jerusalem again.

In her dream, she searches for her lover (3:2). This is similar to the verses in chapter 1 where she did not know where to find her lover (1:7-8). She also mentions her mother again. She is insecure, and when she finds him, she will not let him go (3:4), presumably for fear that she will lose him again. She then gives the same warning to the daughters of Jerusalem again.

5:2-6:2   She has another dream: she asks the daughters of Jerusalem if they find her lover to tell him she is "faint with love"; her friends ask how he is better than others; her answer is simply that his outstanding physical appearance is better than ten thousand others; she admits her lover has gone.

The second dream is similar to the first, except in this one she does not find her lover even after searching for him. Her answer to her friends as to how he is better than other men makes it very clear her love is based mainly upon physical attraction. She is still infatuated with him, but he has gone. This section is again in stark contrast to 3:6 to 5:1 where both Solomon and his bride, and the "girl in a house" with her faithful lover, are described. Both these couples praise each other, and their love is mutual, unlike that of the Shulammite.

When her friends ask where her lover is (6:1) we find out she *does* know where he is. He has "gone down to his garden, to the beds of spices, to browse in the gardens and to gather lilies" (6:2). One commentary (Peake) says this verse "describes with charming allusiveness the union of the bride and bridegroom". I agree it is a discreetly phrased poem to describe consummation, but unfortunately not that of a bride and bridegroom. Here the Shulammite is painfully aware that her unfaithful lover has gone on to pastures new to (euphemistically) "gather lilies". Like the concubine, it seems that she is just one of many women in her lover's life.

Unlike the concubine, however, this is not acceptable to her; on the contrary, it is hurtful. This is once again in stark contrast to the next verse, (6:3) which begins a new section talking about the exclusive and loving relationship between the "girl in the house" and her faithful lover. The suggestion that the break comes between verse 2 and verse 3 is based upon the earlier occurrence of this (almost) exact phrase in 2:16, which forms a part of the poetry relating to the "girl in the house". Both 2:16 and 6:3 say "My lover is mine and I am his" showing a mutual love between the two of them. The section 6:3-10 returns to the "girl in the house" and her faithful lover. His praise for her is a total contrast to the lack of any praise for the Shulammite from her unfaithful lover.

6:11	The Shulammite goes to the vineyards on her own.
6:12	(Possibly says) "before I knew it, I wished I was *in a chariot beside my prince*". (N.B. The experts say this is difficult to translate; words in italics are in *Peake's Commentary*.) Maybe this means that, instead of being alone, she wished that her lover, her "prince", was by her side as he had been in the past.
6:13	The Shulammite has gone away. (This is the *only* verse that refers to her as the "Shulammite" in the entire Song.)

The *New Bible Commentary* considers the Shulammite is speaking in verse 11, not her unfaithful lover. And, as noted above, all commentaries say how difficult verse 12 is to translate. So, possibly what verses 11 and 12 say is that she went down to the grove of nut trees, on her own, to see the vines, and *daydreamed* that she was there with her lover by her side. If she is daydreaming here, it would be consistent with the other sections of poetry about her. She has already *dreamed* of him twice before, as we have seen, and she also *daydreams* about him in chapter 8, as we will see next. However, verse 13 makes it clear that the Shulammite has gone away somewhere, as her friends call her to come back. The last part of verse 13 implies that her unfaithful lover questions why they want to see her, as from 6:1 we saw that he no longer did; he had already gone away himself.

8:1-4   Another daydream: she wishes her lover were like a brother to her so she could take him to her mother's house; she dreams of his physical love; her final warning to the daughters of Jerusalem.

This third and final warning reminds us of the previous two warnings. The daydream ties up with the fact that the Shulammite had two previous dream sequences, and another possible daydream in 6:12. The mention of her mother and her mother's house in this section ties up with two of the earlier sections, including 1:6 which mentions her mother's sons, and 3:4 which mentions her mother's house. Here in this section, although the Shulammite has gone away, she *still* dreams of her unfaithful lover. She finds it very difficult to put him out of her mind. Her warnings of awakening physical love in a man too early are well substantiated by her painful experience of rejection by him, when he went on to pastures new.

| 8:5b | Her unfaithful lover refers to their physical love under the apple tree. (N.B. The *New Bible Commentary* says v 5b refers to physical love; *Jewish Study Bible* says v 5 seems unconnected to the surrounding verses.) |

Verse 5 is difficult to place, as it comprises two separate, and seemingly unconnected phrases. Because of this, I have placed the first half (8:5a) as relating to the "girl in a house" below, and the second half (8:5b) here with the Shulammite. This is based on the fact that the apple tree is mentioned again in 8:5b, which picks up the allusion to this by the Shulammite in 2:3 where she likens her unfaithful lover to an apple tree among the trees of the forest. This fragment of a verse then completes the poetry relating to the Shulammite and her unfaithful lover. Her lover recalls their physical encounter under the apple tree. He points out the similarity to her own mother's encounter under the very same tree, and finishes by saying this was where she had been born. The whole sorry story is completed in half a verse.

What a contrast this is to the supreme happiness between the "girl in the house" and her faithful lover (which we will see below), and with the relative happiness of Solomon and his royal bride, and even with the culturally accepted relationship between the king and the concubine. No wonder this girl, the Shulammite, warned the daughters of Jerusalem *not* to follow in her footsteps.

(3) The royal bride and Solomon

| 3:6-11 | Solomon's carriage comes up from the desert; it's the day of his wedding to his bride from Lebanon. (N.B. Solomon had a splendid court in Lebanon.) |

This section introduces the third couple in the Song – Solomon and his royal bride from Lebanon. There is a great contrast between Solomon and his royal bride, and the relationship between the Shulammite and her unfaithful lover. A large amount of time and money will have been spent by Solomon in preparing beforehand for his marriage to the royal bride, *before* they come together in the physical union of man and wife. This is no casual affair.

This would most likely have been a political alliance in order to achieve long lasting peaceful relations with a foreign country. However, this does not mean the couple have no feelings for one another. It is rather the contrary, as we see when we read the remaining section of poetry about this couple, which beautifully describes their coming together. Although this is most likely an "arranged marriage", there is also a commitment to the relationship. The natural feelings of a man for a woman, and a woman for a man, are described in this bridal love poem.

4:8-5:1   The expression "my sister, my bride" occurs four times; she has stolen his heart; she is a "garden locked up", a "spring enclosed", a "sealed fountain" (a virgin); she asks him to come into her garden; the consummation of their marriage.

The section 4:1-7 is considered to be a *separate* poem to the one in 4:8-5:1 by some commentaries, and I have taken this view. However, some believe *both* poems form a whole, and comprise Solomon's love song to his bride, although they understand that from verse 8 onwards there *is* a subtle change in tone. Thus, they think the whole of chapter 4 and the first verse of chapter 5 are all to do with Solomon and his bride.

However, I believe the first poem in fact relates to the fourth, and final, couple whom we have not yet looked at. This is partly *because* of the subtle change in tone, but also because these first seven verses are very similar to a later poem in the Song which I believe also relates to the fourth, faithful couple.

Here, the royal bride is a virgin before her wedding day, as made clear in verse 12, which in my view clearly distinguishes her from the concubine and the Shulammite. The expression "my sister, my bride" is *only* used in this section, and it is unique in the Song of Songs. This is another reason for thinking it is *only* this section that refers to Solomon and his bride. In my view, this is the only couple in the Song of Songs whose marriage is described. This couple can be compared with the concubine and the king in that it was an acceptable and legal relationship. A royal wife had more status and a much higher position than a concubine, but the security and legality of the relationship was similar.

The beautiful love poem in 4:8-5:1 between Solomon and his bride, however, expresses more depth of feeling than anything said by the king to his concubine in chapter one. Their relationship is closer to the ideal than that of the concubine and the king, and far exceeds the unsatisfactory love affair between the Shulammite and her unfaithful lover. In 4:16 the bride invites the bridegroom to "come into his garden and taste its choice fruits", and in 5:1 Solomon confirms "I have come into my garden, my sister, my bride". The wedding is complete, the marriage is consummated, and the section finishes by saying "Eat, O friends, and drink; drink your fill, O lovers." This couple are left by the Song, happy on their wedding night, with their friends celebrating around them. Compared to the first two couples described above their love is more committed, expressed more deeply, and more honouring to the Lord.

(4) The girl in a house ("a prince's daughter"; "a wall") and her faithful lover

Finally, we come to the fourth couple in the Song of Songs. I refer to her as the "girl in the house" as the first thing we learn about her, in 2:9, is that she can see her lover running up to her house. Then he stands behind her wall, peering through her windows, trying to see if she's in! The very introduction shows us how keen he is to find her, and how she is looking for him expectantly.

2:8-17   This girl's lover leaps like a gazelle to see her; he stands behind the wall of her house; figuratively she herself is a "wall" as we see later in 8:10; he asks her to come away with him; he says he wants to see her face and hear her voice; they have a mutual love one for another – she says "my lover is mine and I am his" (2:16); she also says "until the day breaks and the shadows flee" (2:17) which, later in the Song, is echoed by her lover (4:6); she then asks her lover to be like a gazelle again (2:17) which echoes the beginning, in verse 9.

This girl remembers the words of her faithful lover very clearly and repeats them in this beautiful love poem. The words "my darling, my beautiful one" are used twice in this section and they remind us of earlier in the Song, where the king tells his concubine how beautiful she is, using these same words. These words are used *six times* altogether by the faithful lover in the Song (2:10 & 13; 4:1 & 7; 6:4; 7:6). He is keen to come and see her; he is keen for her to go with him. He can't wait to see her face again and hear her voice. She speaks of their mutual love one for another (2:16), and she repeats this again at the beginning of a later section, in 6:3.

| 4:1-7 | The lover's love song to his bride-to-be; the *New Bible Commentary Revised (1976)* states verses 1-7 are based on a lyric still used in Syrian weddings; it describes the bride's beauty as seen by the bridegroom; her lover repeats the girl's words in 2:17 – "until the day breaks and the shadows flee". |

This pair are betrothed to be married and are waiting for their wedding day. They have fallen in love, and long to be together as much as possible. The section both begins and ends with the lover again repeating "how beautiful you are, my darling! Oh, how beautiful!" again linking this section to the previous one. As mentioned above, these words form part of a lyric used in Syrian weddings, so perhaps it is not surprising they are repeated a number of times throughout the Song.

A number of the lover's descriptions of the girl here are repeated in two later sections of the Song. Her hair is like a flock of goats (4:1) comes again in 6:5. Her teeth are like a flock of sheep (v2) comes again in 6:6. Her temples are like the halves of a pomegranate (v3) comes again in 6:7. Her neck is like a tower (v4) comes again in 7:4. Her breasts are like twin fawns (v5) comes again in 7:3. These two later sections (in chapters 6 and 7) echo this section, and also add further extravagant and complimentary descriptions of her beauty and perfection in his eyes.

Many commentaries recognise that a new section of poetry starts at verse 8 (e.g. *Peake* and the *New Bible Commentary Revised*). The *New Bible Commentary Revised* states "certainly there is a different tone to these verses compared with the first half of the chapter."

| 6:3-10 | The girl repeats the words "I am my lover's and my lover is mine" (from 2:16) linking this section to the earlier one where the "girl in the house" speaks; her lover responds with another beautiful love poem in verses 4-9; she is his perfect one, she is unique, the maidens call her blessed and queens and concubines praise her; her lover starts the poem in this section by saying she is as "awesome as bannered hosts" and his friends finish the poem by echoing these *exact* words (in the *Jewish Tanakh* and *Young's Literal* translations). |

I have started this section at verse 3 because it then connects to the *end* of the earlier section in 2:8-17, where the girl also uses this phrase in respect of her and her lover. This results in a flowing continuity of thoughts. I have ended this section at verse 10 because here the faithful lover's friends echo the exact words that he uses to start his description of the girl, in verse 4.

The words "you are beautiful, my darling" are stated again in this section (v4), for the fifth time by the faithful lover. As mentioned earlier, he repeats this phrase six times in the Song, and each of these echoes the first occurrence in 1:15. His descriptions of her also echo those in chapter 4, as we have already seen. Her hair is like a flock of goats, her teeth like a flock of sheep and her temples like the halves of a pomegranate.

| 7:1-13 | Her lover praises her with another love song; he describes her as "a prince's daughter"; some of the details are similar to those in 4:1-7 as above (e.g. 4:5 and 7:3 – breasts like fawns; 4:4 and 7:4 – neck like a tower); he looks forward to the future consummation of their love in 7:8 (*Peake's* |

Commentary); she promises her love to him (v12); she has stored up her love for him (v13); this couple have clearly *not* consummated their love.

This section has two parts. First the faithful lover praises the girl with another poem, which is very similar, in part, to the previous two sections which we have looked at above. Verses 3 and 4 in particular are a refrain of what we read in 4:4-5. The girl then responds to what he has said, and looks forward, discreetly, to the consummation of their relationship in marriage (as suggested by *Peake's Commentary*).

8:5a The first half of verse 5 says:
"Who is this coming up from the desert leaning on her lover?"

The *Jewish Study Bible* says 8:5 seems unconnected to the surrounding verses. It is difficult to place this verse, especially as it falls into two distinct and separate halves. The first half almost repeats 3:6 word for word, where Solomon the bridegroom came up from the desert in his carriage. Maybe here it refers to the "girl in the house" leaning on her faithful lover? Maybe the link is that she *seems* like a royal bride to him? After all, he does refer to her as a "prince's daughter" in 7:1. Maybe it serves as an introduction to verses 6 and 7?

(N.B. See earlier for 8:5b, in the section on the Shulammite and her unfaithful lover.)

8:6-7 The bride-to-be gives a moving description of love; "love is as strong as death"; "it burns like blazing fire"; "rivers cannot wash it away"; it is unquenchable and unpurchaseable.

The *Jewish Tanakh* says "these verses are unique in the poem because they deal with love in the abstract". *Peake's Commentary* says "for a moment we stand apart from the movement of the poem and reflect on the real nature of love that so completely unites man and woman."

These two verses form the pinnacle of the entire Song. They are recognised as a separate and unique part of the Song, and that is why I have separated them from the second part of verse 5, which as explained above, is considered to be a "fragment" in the Song, and difficult to place.

This beautiful description of human love talks about a love that never dies, and lasts until death. It is a love that is priceless and can never be bought. It is given freely without any thought of receiving anything in return. This is the girl's response to the love shown to her by her faithful lover. Love begets love. This is a love that encompassed her completely – body, mind and spirit.

8:8-14   The "wall" refers to chastity and the "door" refers to easy virtue (8:9); the girl in the house is "a wall" (chaste); (her *literal* wall is mentioned in 2:9); she brings peace and contentment because she can be trusted to be faithful; love that is purchased is compared with love that is given freely; the lover wants to hear her voice (a repeat of 2:14); she asks her lover to be like a gazelle (a repeat of 2:9 and 2:17).

These final seven verses complete the Song of Songs. Some consider these verses an anti-climax after reading verses 6 and 7. However, I see it as bringing the Song of Songs to a gentle and loving conclusion. There is the contrast between chastity and easy virtue (verse 9). There is the contrast between Solomon with his wealth and his harem, and the true love between a man and a woman, the love that cannot be bought (vs 11-12).

It then finishes with two repetitions from the first section in chapter 2 where the loving and faithful couple are first introduced; the faithful lover longs to hear her voice (2:14) and the girl asks him to "be like a gazelle or like a young stag on the spice-laden mountains" (2:9, 17). And so this faithful couple finish the Song, the one couple out of the four that give a wonderful example of the Lord's perfect plan for love between men and women.

Conclusion

Conclusion

As I said earlier, and it bears repeating here, the Song is not only an incomparable piece of literature on human love. it also serves as a warning to women not to "arouse love before it so desires". This is stated three times throughout the Song, and it is clearly an important part of the message that the writer wished to convey. Women will often be hurt and disillusioned by men if they arouse expectations in them and consummate their love early in their relationship.

Some men, who act like the kings in the OT with their harems, will go from woman to woman, leaving the women to regret encouraging such a relationship. To the man this may be based (mostly) on physical attraction, and may not involve any thought of marriage, or of a long-term relationship at all. On the other hand, women will be esteemed and respected by men if they remain chaste before their wedding day, like the royal bride with King Solomon, and like the "girl in the house". The physical attraction is still very much there, but it is consummated at the right time, on the wedding night.

Physical attraction between men and women is not wrong, but the Song of Songs in the Bible warns that the consummation of this should be unique between one man and one woman, reserved for one monogamous relationship of mutual love and trust. In this context, physical love between a man and a woman is seen to be a beautiful thing, designed by God and resulting in a totally unique relationship, different from all others, throughout the couple's life. The couple become, and remain, truly "one" in the eyes of God (Genesis 2:24; Matthew 19:5). The Song of Songs is not only relevant to the age in which it was written, but, as human nature does not change over the centuries, I believe it is just as relevant today.

More on
The Song of Songs

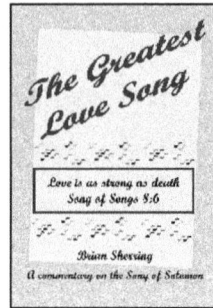

**The Greatest Love Song:
A commentary on the Song of Solomon
By Brian Sherring**

**Song of Songs:
An introduction and its relevance for today
By Brian Sherring**

Further details of these books mentioned be seen on
www.obt.org.uk

They can also be ordered from that website and also from:
The Open Bible Trust,
Fordland Mount, Upper Basildon,
Reading, RG8 8LU, UK.

They are also available as eBooks from Amazon and Apple
and as KDP paperbacks from Amazon.

About the Author

Sylvia Penny was born in Bexleyheath, Kent, in 1956. She was educated at Basingstoke High School and Queen Mary's College, before studying accountancy at Oxford Polytechnic. She qualified as a Chartered Accountant and practised in the profession for a number of years, until she went to live in the USA with her husband and was a pastor's wife, taking an active role in the church. On returning to Britain she went back to the accountancy profession and now works part time as an accountant.

She is a regular contributor to *Search* magazine and has written a number of Bible Study Booklets. She has also written the following major books:

- Satan through the Bible
- Salvation: Safe and Secure
- Woman to Woman (which she compiled and edited)
- Introducing God's Plan (written with Michael Penny)
- Abraham and his seed (written with William Henry and Michael Penny

Also by Sylvia Penny

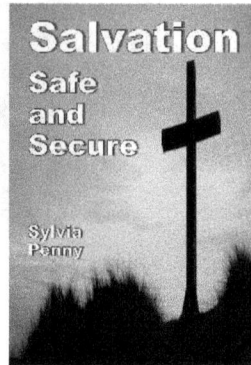

Woman to Woman

Compiled and edited by Sylvia Penny

Sixty articles by women and for women, covering such subjects as:

- Old Testament Women
- New Testament Women
- Roman and Greek Women
- Jesus and Women
- Paul and Women
- Husbands & Wives
- Raising Children.
- Christian Living
- Modern Day Issues

A great book for women's ministry.

Salvation: Safe and Secure?

By Sylvia Penny

This important book is a thorough treatment of the subject of salvation, asking such questions as …

- ☐ What is it, exactly, that saves us?
- ☐ Is salvation secure?
- ☐ Can it be lost?
- ☐ What is 'conditional security'?

It deals with a wide number of issues such as …

- Salvation and works
- The doctrine of rewards
- Lordship salvation
- Free grace theology
- Assurance of salvation
- Why people lose their faith

Further details of these books mentioned be seen on

www.obt.org.uk

They can also be ordered from that website and also from:

The Open Bible Trust,
Fordland Mount, Upper Basildon,
Reading, RG8 8LU, UK.

They are also available as eBooks from Amazon and Apple and as KDP paperbacks from Amazon.

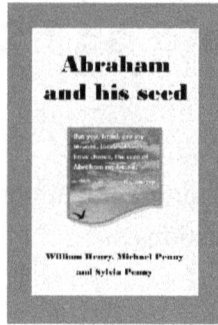

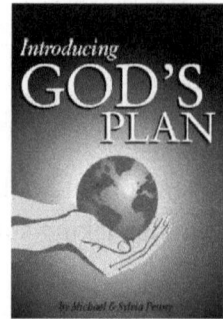

Satan through the Bible
By Sylvia Penny

Abraham and his seed
By William Henry, Michael Penny and Sylvia Penny

Introducing God's Plan
By Sylvia and Michael Penny

About this Book

Song of Songs
An Alternative View

Much has been written about the Song of Songs over the centuries and theories abound as to its true meaning. One of the keys to understanding this book, however, is that it is poetry, so there are repetitions and refrains throughout, and these need to be taken into account if we are to understand what is being said, and why it is included in Scripture.

Is it a story told, in poetic form, of a man and a woman deeply in love, in a monogamous relationship, possibly betrothed, waiting for their wedding day? Or is it describing the relationships of four different women with four different men - one a king, one Solomon, one an unfaithful lover, and one a faithful lover? It is this last scenario that this book considers.

Publications of The Open Bible Trust must be in accordance with its evangelical, fundamental and dispensational basis. However, beyond this minimum, writers are free to express whatever beliefs they may have as their own understanding, provided that the aim in so doing is to further the object of The Open Bible Trust. A copy of the doctrinal basis is available on **www.obt.org.uk** or from:

THE OPEN BIBLE TRUST
Fordland Mount, Upper Basildon,
Reading, RG8 8LU, UK

www.ingramcontent.com/pod-product-compliance
Lightning Source LLC
Chambersburg PA
CBHW060619030426
42337CB00018B/3121